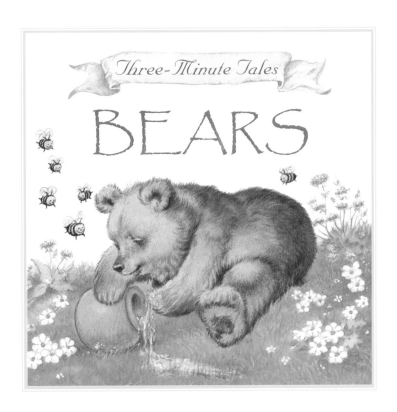

Three-Minute Tales

BEARS

p

This is a Parragon book
First Published in 2000

Parragon
Queen Street House, 4 Queen Street,
Bath, BA1 1HE, UK

Produced by The Templar Company plc
Pippbrook Mill, London Road, Dorking,
Surrey, RH4 1JE, UK

Designed by Kilnwood Graphics

Printed and bound in Spain
ISBN 0 75255 638 X

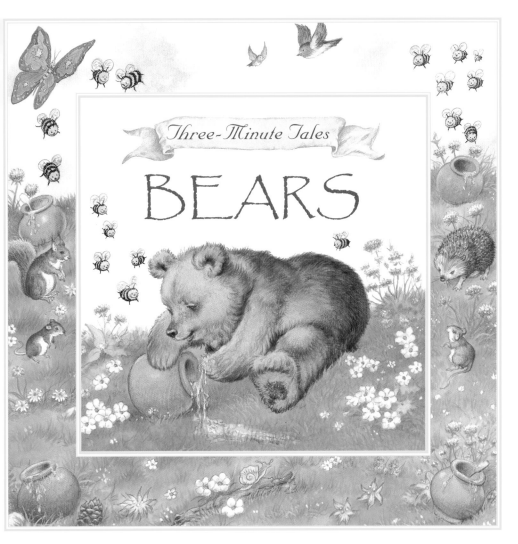

Three-Minute Tales

BEARS

Written by Caroline Repchuk • Illustrated by Mario Capaldi

CONTENTS

One Snowy Day

The Smart Bear
and the Foolish Bear

HONEY BEAR
AND THE BEES

One day, as Honey Bear woke from her dreams,
her furry little nose started to twitch with
excitement. She could smell her favourite
thing in the world — sweet, yummy honey!
The smell was coming from a hollow tree stump
nearby. She padded over and dipped in a large
paw. How delicious the sweet, sticky honey tasted!

Honey Bear dipped her paw in again and
again, digging deep into the tree stump to
reach more of the lovely sticky honey.
This was the life! In fact, she dug so deep

that when she tried to take her great paw out,
she found it was stuck fast! Just then, she heard
a loud buzzing noise and looked up to see a huge
swarm of angry bees returning to their hive!

Poor Honey Bear hollered as the bees
flew around, stinging her all over! She tugged
and tugged and at last she pulled her paw free.
The angry bees chased her all the way to the
river where she sat cooling her burning skin.
Just then an irresistible smell reached her furry
nose. It was coming from a hollow tree nearby.
"Mmm, honey!" said Honey Bear. "I'll just go
and take a look!.."

Baby Bear
Finds a Friend

Baby Bear stretched as he woke from his long
winter sleep. He took a deep breath of fresh
spring air and smiled at the warm sun on his
back. He was bursting with energy. Now all
he needed was someone to play with.
"Come and play with me," he called to Owl.
"I only play at night!" said Owl, sleepily.

Nearby some little bunnies were playing. Baby
Bear bounded over to join the fun, but Mrs
Rabbit shooed him away. "Your paws will hurt
my babies," she said. "You can't play with them."

Next he climbed up to see if Squirrel would
play with him, but Squirrel told him to go
away. "I'm trying to make a nest," said Squirrel,
crossly, "and you are shaking the tree!"

Baby Bear wandered down to the river, where
some beavers were hard at work building a dam.
"Come and play with me," called Baby Bear.
But the beavers were too busy. So he sat
watching Kingfisher diving into the water.
"That looks like fun!" he said, jumping in
with a splash! "Go away!" said Kingfisher.
"You're disturbing the fish!"

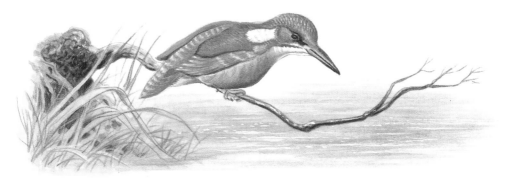

By now Baby Bear was feeling fed up and tired. He lay down in a hollow and closed his eyes. Then, just as he was drifting to sleep, a voice said, "Will you come and play with me?"

He opened his eyes to see another bear cub.
Baby Bear smiled. "I'm too tired to play now,"
he said. "But I'll play with you tomorrow!"
And from then on, he was never lonely again.

ONE SNOWY DAY

One snowy day, Old Bear poked his nose out
of his den, and looked at the deep snow that
had fallen while he slept. "I'll take a stroll in the
woods," he said. Off he went, his great paws
padding along, as big white snowflakes tickled
his nose. How he loved the snow! He walked
far into the woods, deep in thought, and quite
forgot to look where he was going.

After a while, Old Bear stopped and looked around. To his dismay, he realised he was quite lost. Then he spied the trail of pawprints behind him. "Ho, ho!" he chuckled. "I'm not lost at all! I can follow my pawprints home!"

And thinking what a clever old bear he was, he carried on walking, until at last he began to feel tired. " I'll just take a rest," he said to himself. He closed his eyes, and soon fell fast asleep. Meanwhile, the snow kept on falling...

By the time Old Bear woke up his trail of pawprints had disappeared! "Now I'll never find my way home!" he groaned. Then, he noticed an old tree stump nearby. "That looks familiar. And so does that fallen log over there. If I'm not mistaken, I've walked in a big circle, and ended up at home!" he chuckled, turning towards his den. "What a clever old bear I am, after all!"

THE SMART BEAR AND THE FOOLISH BEAR

It was the start of winter. The first snow had fallen, and the lake had begun to freeze. It was nearly time for all the bears to start their winter sleep. But there was one foolish bear who wasn't ready to sleep yet. "I'll just catch one more fish," he told himself, "to keep me going through winter." And although he knew it was dangerous, he crept out onto the icy lake.

He lay down on his tummy, and broke a hole
in the ice. He could see lots of fish swimming
in the water below. He dipped his paw into
the hole, and scooped out a fish in a flash!

But the foolish little bear was so excited he leapt up, shouting, "I caught one!" With a great crack, the ice gave way beneath him, and he fell into the freezing water!

Luckily a smart little bear cub heard his cries, and rushed to help. He found a fallen log and pushed it over the ice. The foolish bear grabbed it, and pulled himself to safety, still holding the fish. "How can I thank you?" he asked. "That fish would do nicely," said the smart little bear, and he strolled away to start his winter's sleep.

The End